Quantum Listening

Quantum Listening

PAULINE OLIVEROS

Published in 2024 by Spiral House, an imprint of Silver Press.

First published in this single edition in 2022 by Ignota (2018-2024), a press created by Sarah Shin and Ben Vickers. Ignota's archive can be found at ignota.org.

'Quantum Listening' by Pauline Oliveros was first published in *Sounding the Margins*, 2010.
Reprinted by permission of Pauline Oliveros Publications and The Ministry of Maåt, Inc.

ISBN: 978-1-7393717-5-3

Design by Rose Nordin
Typeset in Adobe Caslon Pro by Marsha Swan
Printed in the UK by TJ Books, Padstow, Cornwall

1 3 5 7 9 10 8 6 4 2

Contents

Foreword

Quantum Listening is Full of Space and Questions

BY LAURIE ANDERSON

When I think of Pauline I think of laughing. I'm picturing us in a hot tub in Telluride, Colorado; must have been some time in the nineties. It was getting dark and we were tipping our heads back, looking up at the mountains and making puns that got sillier and sillier. This particular evening, we'd just done a public talk about 'sound in film' and were laughing about some of the pompous, unlikely things we'd said. I can't really hear our voices. It's more like I remember certain scenes.

For a few years Pauline and I were both working at EMPAC, a big experimental media and performance art center in Troy, New York. I'm thinking of a performance we did there together: she was playing the accordion and I spent the whole concert kneeling on the floor trying to reprogram a system on my laptop. Occasionally I'd look up and she would nod at me, wordless, as though to say, 'Take your time! I'll just be sitting over here, playing.' I never fixed the problem with the laptop. When the concert ended, no one mentioned I hadn't played a note.

A couple of months after this concert, Pauline got in touch with me to say she would be doing a talk and could arrange some tickets for me, in case it sold out. She said, 'I'm really chuffed about this and hope you can come.' When I got there, the auditorium was closed. I thought: maybe I have the wrong night. I went upstairs to her office. There was a light under the door, and I knocked and pushed it open.

'Hey, hi!' I said. 'What happened to the show?'

'Actually . . . nobody showed up. But I am so chuffed about this idea!' She spent the next two hours showing me charts and playing sounds, doing the lecture just for me.

Pauline was a Quantum Listener and this essay is a collection of questions (When do you stop hearing the sound? When does memory begin? How does Mars sound?); suggestions (zoom into a waterfall to hear individual drops); inventions (listen to your blood to monitor your health); aphorisms (the ear tells the eye where to look); observations (there is no courting of silence) and advice (remind yourself when you are not listening). It's full of stories about technology, hybrid humans, spirituality, physicality and the Chip Monk.

Spatial sound

My tai chi teacher begins each session with the words, 'Listen behind you.' It always makes me think of Pauline. Recently, after decades of loud sounds and city living, I've lost some of my hearing at higher frequencies, so I bought some hearing aids. They have a function that allows you to listen behind you, handy for restaurant eavesdropping.

As a tai chi practitioner, I've felt the electric charge when the palms pass each other – what Pauline described as 'listening with the palms of the hands'. I have to think further about her ideas on what happens to qi when it condenses. I've done many concerts featuring drones – the name we gave to the feedback of eight-to-twelve of Lou Reed's guitars set up as installations lasting for six hours – and I'm convinced that listening to them, especially while doing tai chi, taps into an otherworldly healing energy.

Quantum Listening is not really a Buddhist exercise

But like Buddhism, Deep Listening puts experience before everything else. It emphasizes both detail and scope of, in Pauline's words, 'the sounds of daily life, of nature, or one's own thoughts'.

'We're not a nation of listeners,' she wrote. To say the least! Deep Listening is inside your head and empathetic. Both focal and global.

And Stevie Wonder too

A few years ago I was at the Rock and Roll Hall of Fame Induction Ceremony. I was sitting at a big table near the stage and the awards ceremony was dragging on and on. I was writing and rewriting my speech. After three hours, the printed text was mostly crossed out and my tiny handwriting snaked up the margins, punctuated by stars, dashes and arrows, pointing to smaller scraps of paper that were attached by tight folds to the main pages.

A lot of people were scheduled to give speeches, but there seemed to be no running order. You only knew at the last second when you'd be called. The stage manager would run over to your table, his headset crackling, and mouth, 'You're next!'

Stevie Wonder sat across from me at the table. He was alone – with no manager or friend. He was turning his head around and around in small circles, almost like a radar. Once every half hour or so, the stage manager would tap him on the shoulder, guide him to the stage to play, and then guide him back to the table.

As the hours crept by, people kept coming over to Stevie's table. Like most awards ceremonies, this one was a hobnobbing, see-and-be-seen scene, so people were waving across the room, 'Hey hey come over here!' and table-hopping 'Oh man, you look soooo good! How you been? Congrats on that Grammy, man!'

People came up to Stevie pretty often and all at once I realized what that must be like. He couldn't see them coming, waving their way towards him from across the room. They were just suddenly in his ear, inside his head. 'Stevie man, it's Clive! How you been?' Or, 'Stevie dude, you don't remember me but we met in '84 on the road.' Maybe he'd get a brief warning – a smell of aftershave or perfume. But for the most part, they just appeared without warning.

In other words

I work with an AI program whose algorithms are based on everything I've published and recorded. So it speaks with my vocabulary, syntax and, let's say, style. For fun and a little collaboration I entered Pauline's line, 'In the twenty-first century, we will be grappling with who we are as extended humans.'

Here's what the program came up with:

> By the end of the movie, we'll all be sitting around in the twenty-first century with our heads as low as we can get.
>
> Where are we? Are we out of cigarettes? Or do we just smoke once and leave it at that? In the twentieth century, there were more humans on the streets than animals. Now, it's not so surprising: they're here all the time.
>
> Why don't you listen to me?
>
> I'm the only one left who knows how to talk to God.
>
> You know, I should really get a studio – do some commercials. You know it would be so much fun. They'd be able to play so many different songs – right down to who is pissing and who is tickling or brushing or blowing a fuse or getting their shoes laid or going to the store. Or just standing around watching the world go by. And who are these people – these grappling hooks?
>
> Human beings do things no one else can do. For instance, they go to war. And then come out on the other side.
>
> The computer says: No And I say: Well, where do you want to go? Or what's for supper? Get me back down to the sea. Can't you see I'm full of human beings?

Laurie Anderson

March 2022

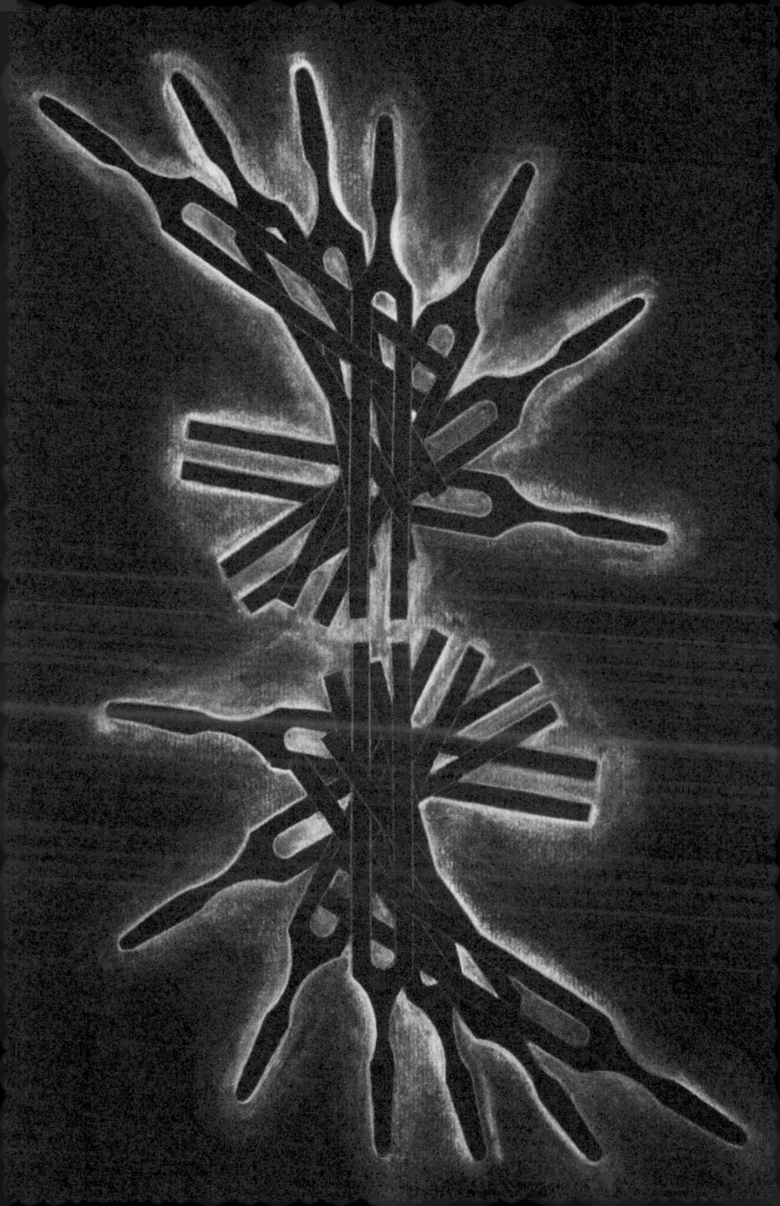

Introduction

As I Write, I Listen

BY IONE

'As you listen, the particles of sound decide to be heard. Listening affects what is sounding.

It is a symbiotic relationship. As you listen, the environment is enlivened.

This is the listening effect.'[1]

As I write, I listen

The words forming in my mind are sounds.

Listening forward in time, I sense and feel you: the reader, listening as well.

By listening in this manner I am experiencing 'the listening effect', which not only transports me, but simultaneously centers me in the present moment.

1. Unless stated otherwise, the quotes throughout this introduction are from Pauline Oliveros' published work, including *Deep Listening Pieces* (1990), *Deep Listening: A Composer's Sound Practice* (2005), *Sounding the Margins: Collected Writings 1992–2009* (2010) and *Anthology of Text Scores* (2013), all published by Deep Listening Publications.

My listening continues to deepen and expand as I practice Pauline Oliveros' lifelong passion, Deep Listening.[2]

Quantum theory is such an integral part of Pauline's teachings, that she might well have used this title to encompass the bulk of her teachings. But the term Deep Listening took root not long after the moment in 1988 when Pauline, Stuart Dempster and Panaiotis descended into the Dan Harpole Cistern, a long, empty receptacle for water fourteen feet underground, built by the US Military near Seattle, Washington. In the cavernous depths, they listened intently as their sounds returned to them with an extraordinary delay of forty-five seconds. As an afterthought they brought along recording equipment, resulting in the 1989 album *Deep Listening*. Both Pauline and Stuart were notorious punsters, and titling the album 'Deep Listening' made them smile and laugh out loud.

2. Deep Listening®, as developed by Pauline Oliveros, explores the difference between the involuntary nature of hearing and the voluntary, selective nature of listening.

As I listen, I remember

> '*Futurist: Adj: relating to a vision of the future, especially one involving the development of technology.*' —Oxford Dictionaries

Winter 1999. The century was ending and a new one beginning. Pauline, increasingly known as a 'futurist', was invited to give the plenary speech at the International Congress on Culture and Humanity in the New Millennium: The Future of Human Values at the Chinese University of Hong Kong. I had witnessed Pauline composing it on her laptop in the chair across from me in the sitting room, and now I listened in the audience as she gave the greeting in Mandarin she had learned for the occasion, and then presented her paper: 'Quantum Listening: From Practice to Theory (To Practice Practice).'

As I write and listen, hidden sounds emerge

Tourists were laughing and chattering in many languages. We were happy to be tourists too, on our first trip to Hong Kong, where Pauline's speech was well received by the attentive audience.

We took a ferry to get to Ngong Ping, in the western part of Lantau Island, to see the Big Buddha. The statue –

112 feet tall and constructed of 202 bronze pieces – made for an imposing sculpture rising high into the sky. From a distance, gazing at the steps leading to the top, we wondered if we could make it all the way up the 268 steps to reach the Buddha. But once in motion, like much else in our lives, there was never a question of turning back.

As I write and listen now to these *remembered sounds* of our fellow tourists, mixed with the sounds of our own footsteps and our own breathing, previously unheard sounds emerge in my consciousness. Was there a sonic camaraderie that boosted our energy for the climb? Or perhaps, as we sensed near the top, this energy emanated from the Big Buddha's extended palm directly above us.

Until now, I had not consciously recalled these airy, joyful, climbing sounds, but somehow they are still here with me.

As I write, I listen to Hong Kong again

> *'In practicing qi gong I have experienced listening with the palms of my hands to sense these magnetic waves.'*

Spring 2013. Returning to Hong Kong was like a quantum leap. On our second visit, we did not climb to the top of the

Big Buddha again, but he was a strong presence from the air on our arrival, as well as our departure.

Pauline was to perform a solo concert on the rooftop of an elegant building. The audience had quietly gathered and were waiting for her to begin. Then, there it was. I listened to the snap of her opening her instrument, and then the sound of her accordion breathing – her trademark opening, so simple and so powerful.

Her long chords began to fill the air, and they were odd, surprising, yet familiar – for they were coming from us. We formed an intrinsic part of the roots of that moment.

Behind her, the presenters had arranged a surprise fireworks display. She did not turn to see them, but it was clear that she felt and sensed their presence.

We all listened with Pauline as the distant sounds of hissing, whistling and crackling of the fireworks mingled with her music. They became an integral part of it. They listened to her and she to them and we, the audience, were a part of that listening field. It was comforting. It was enlivening. Our ears witnessed the quantum effect.

In 1976, our friend, composer and sinologist R. I. P. Hayman, conducted experiments at the Sleep Research Laboratories at the Montefiore Medical Center, New

York. These early experiments, as well as more recent scientific studies, show that the tympanic membrane of the ear, commonly known as the eardrum, responds to the sounds in our dreams.[3]

I take this as tangible evidence of an organic Deep Listening mechanism within our physiology. This membrane must also respond to 'imagined sounds' and 'remembered sounds', since both forms are accessed by 'inter-dimensional listening', which is very close to listening in dreams.

Pauline's extensive Imaginary Meditations were intended to open up this vast field of sound for us. A slip of paper, dated 1997, fell out of a book and caught my attention in an incident that physicist and therapist Arnold Mindell would call a 'quantum flirt'. Pauline's handwritten notes for a class she was teaching read:

Can You Imagine?
Tiny footsteps
Children laughing
A door opening
Water running over rocks
A horse galloping

3. R. I. P. Hayman's 'Listening to Dreams: Project for Inner Ear Muscle Activity Audio Level Telemetry' is included in my book *Listening in Dreams: A Compendium of Sound Dreams, Meditations and Rituals for Deep Dreamers*, iUniverse, 2005.

Fire burning in the fireplace
The telephone ringing
Your favorite music
A church bell ringing
The sound of your voice
A dog barking
Loud applause from an audience
A motor cycle late at night
A bird song in the morning
Wind in the tree leaves
An owl calling

I am listening from 2000 miles away

> *'Listening Performers experience the Listening Effect as they are performing for the audience'*

In February 2022, the durational show *Lifes* opened at the Hammer Museum in Los Angeles. The original plan was for me to be present and perform live at the opening, but a renewed viral scare meant that instead I performed from my office in Hudson Valley, New York. I was visible and audible on a giant, wall-sized screen as, at the request of the curator, the track 'IONE' on the *Deep Listening* album played to the group of people gathered in a large, comfortable room with soft, wall-to-wall carpeting. I invited them to relax and to recline, if they were so disposed, while they listened. This Deep Listening exercise was a prelude, a 'tune up' for us, before I invited all to participate in Pauline's 'Tuning Meditation' with their own voices.

I have facilitated the 'Tuning Meditation' many times in various versions – live with a live audience, streamed, with an audience as virtual as me ... This time, I was struck by how moved I was by the sensation of being with them and with Pauline's music, in this ever-so-slightly different form of virtual communication. My performance comprised *listening to their listening,* as well as to my own. Something special, something both old and new, had occurred. Something healing. The mystery of a non-local quantum moment out of time, demonstrating Pauline's message that *practiced listening* continues to evolve, consistently yielding new information.

Listing 8,000 feet up

'The wilderness world listens to itself even today.' —Yaqui Deer Song[4]

We held the first Deep Listening retreat in 1991 at a small retreat center in the Sangre de Cristo Mountains, 8,000 feet above Las Vegas, New Mexico. Over the following two decades Pauline would return many times, solidifying her relationship to Deep Listening and to the wonderful students. Performance artist, choreographer and tai chi and qi gong instructor Heloise Gold brought her special movement and the Tao to us; and I brought an exploration of 'the dream of reality and the reality of the dream' – with the practice of awareness of sound in dreams and 24-hour listening.

Between teaching sessions, Pauline would meditate for long periods of time up on the rocks. One day she returned to us beaming, for a tiny hummingbird had found her sitting on a huge rock in her red-orange T-shirt. After some consideration, as if studying the situation, the bird had buzzed near her heart three times, before settling upon her chest and looking directly into her eyes.

I listen now, through memory, as Pauline intones:

4. From 'Deer Dancer', *Yaqui Deer Songs/Maso Bwikam: A Native American Poetry* by Larry Evers and Felipe S. Molina, University of Arizona Press, 1987.

'Brrrrrrr! Brrrrrr! Brrrrrr!' A pause and then, again: 'Brrrrrr! Brrrrrr! Brrrrrr! Brrrrrr! Brrrrrr! Brrrrrr!'

Brimming over with laughter, she joyfully mimicked the sound of the sturdy little wings, demonstrating the power of her hummingbird 'medicine'. That week, she mostly explored healing with humming; it is only now that I recognize Pauline's sounds as identical to the sounds she made when presenting and performing one of her signature meditations. In her piece 'Sounds from Childhood', she suggests:

> *There was likely a time in your childhood when it was really fun to make sounds – especially the ones that adults admonished you for making.*
>
> *Listen and remember when you loved to make sounds as a child and relax with the feelings.*
>
> In the next few minutes, choose three to five of those sounds to make.
>
> *Let's begin with a nice deep breath – and exhale the air audibly.*
>
> *On the next inhale prepare, then make your first sound on the exhale.*
>
> *Continue by listening for a space for your sounds before, after, or with someone else's sound.*
>
> *Enjoy!*

As I write, I listen to sounds from Ukraine

'A Quantum Listener encompasses the entire field of sound as well as the focal point.'

The sounds of war emanating from the television in the sitting room and from the radio in the kitchen are the antithesis of Pauline's intention for the world. At the same time, the percussive sounds of jackhammers drift across the distance toward my ears. They are repairing the old bridge that crosses Rondout Creek near my home. I do not mind the mechanical noise and prefer it to sounds that might manifest should the old bridge be torn down. I listen to the jackhammers and the sounds of war simultaneously, opening up the density of the focal listening and the expansiveness of the global listening. It is through this practice of listening, in a heightened state of awareness, that I am able to affect the listening field and bear witness to war. It is through listening that transformation is possible.

As I listen, the sounds of war are not eradicated, but some despair in me – and in the world at large, perhaps – is lifting. More energy is made available for harmonious action, whether emanating from body or mind.

I am reminded that we humans have restorative skills as well as ignorant and destructive ones. I am reminded not to forget this as I interact in the world. I remember that Pauline's listening practices enhance openness. Imagining Deep Listening spreading throughout the world brings comfort.

> *'Compassion (spiritual development) and understanding comes from listening impartially to the whole space/time of sound impartially, not just what one is presently concerned about.'*

I am listening for a Dynamic Peace

Pauline started developing her groundbreaking Sonic Meditations with members of the ♀ Ensemble in the late 1960s, in response to the Vietnam War and what she called the general 'atmosphere of war, of protest, of resistance'. After the self-immolation of George Winne Jr. at the University of California, San Diego, where she taught, she experienced a 'withdrawal to introspection, and listening introspectively'.

The Sonic Meditations were also to enable 'people to be able to have significant experiences with sound in a communal way'. It was clear to Pauline that participants in this dedicated community experienced a sense of well-being and relaxation from the practices. This experiment in intense sounding and listening was instrumental to her development of a practice and a body of work that is inclusive, welcoming and accessible to the musically trained and non-musicians alike.

Deeply affected by conflict and war, she began to describe her music-making as being intended for expanding consciousness and for 'humanitarian purposes; specifically healing', dedicating many of her scores and concerts to 'an end to violence'. 'The Sonic Meditations were my response to the war,' she explained.

Can you imagine the tuning of the world?

Pauline's 'Tuning Meditation' can be performed by anywhere from two or three people to thousands. Intended for healing, a new, living entity is sonically formed each time the meditation is performed. Pauline's last transmission of this piece in person occurred in London at St John's Church in Smith Square, Westminster. The performance took place in June 2016, as the historic vote on Brexit resulted in the news that the UK was leaving the European Union. Many in the audience were stunned and upset and needing solace. Pauline directed the score from the stage for over 500 people, whose voices rose and fell. The audience–performers sang, with much feeling-finding, a tone in their own 'minds' ear' and alternately tuned to another tone in the room or contributed a new tone that no one else was singing. They sang warmly, following her instructions to fill the cathedral to the vaulted ceiling and ended beautifully, completely in unison.

There was to be another powerful moment when this piece met a worldly need. During April 2020, in the first months of the novel coronavirus pandemic, I presented the 'World Wide Tuning Meditation' each week on Zoom, in collaboration with conductor, musician and visual artist Raquel Acevedo Klein's Music on the Rebound, flutist and MacArthur Fellow Claire Chase, and the International Contemporary Ensemble. The events reached more than 4,600 participants from all seven continents and over thirty countries.

As the performances were underway, I realized that we were manifesting Pauline's futuristic vision. After many performances with hundreds, some with thousands, of people present, Pauline had dreamed of a truly worldwide version. I could feel her smiling with delight when we embraced this technology in order to impart a sense of meaning and connection, even a sense of love, over distance. Many had had qualms and doubts about the use of the internet but were surprised and even converted by the amount of feeling and love that was transmitted via this medium. The 'World Wide Tuning Meditation' series was a swift response to the global crisis and an affirmation of Pauline's vision of a harmonious world community.

Pauline has given inspiration and instructions through the depth of her listening. Her music is still resonating in quantum universes. We receive guidance from her books and essays, her keynote addresses and talks. Her graphic scores are our guiding maps.

Pauline's *Quantum Listening* is a clearly worded manifesto advocating for the practice of Deep Listening – the practice of practice. Accessing both the focal and the global at once makes us Futurists too, both creators and recipients of the newness, the peace and the health we long for.

A champion of the underserved and underrepresented, Pauline dares us to embrace change, the unfamiliar and even the unknown. She wants us to be bold enough to imagine a benevolent society that can embrace technology to create a sublime music.

'Yes,' she writes, 'Deep Listening is a foundation for a radically transformed social matrix in which compassion and love are the core motivating principles guiding creative decision making and our actions in the world.'

Through Quantum Listening – listening to listening – we can realize a new music and a new world – if we can listen deeply enough with Pauline.

Can you imagine listening beyond the edge of your own imagination?

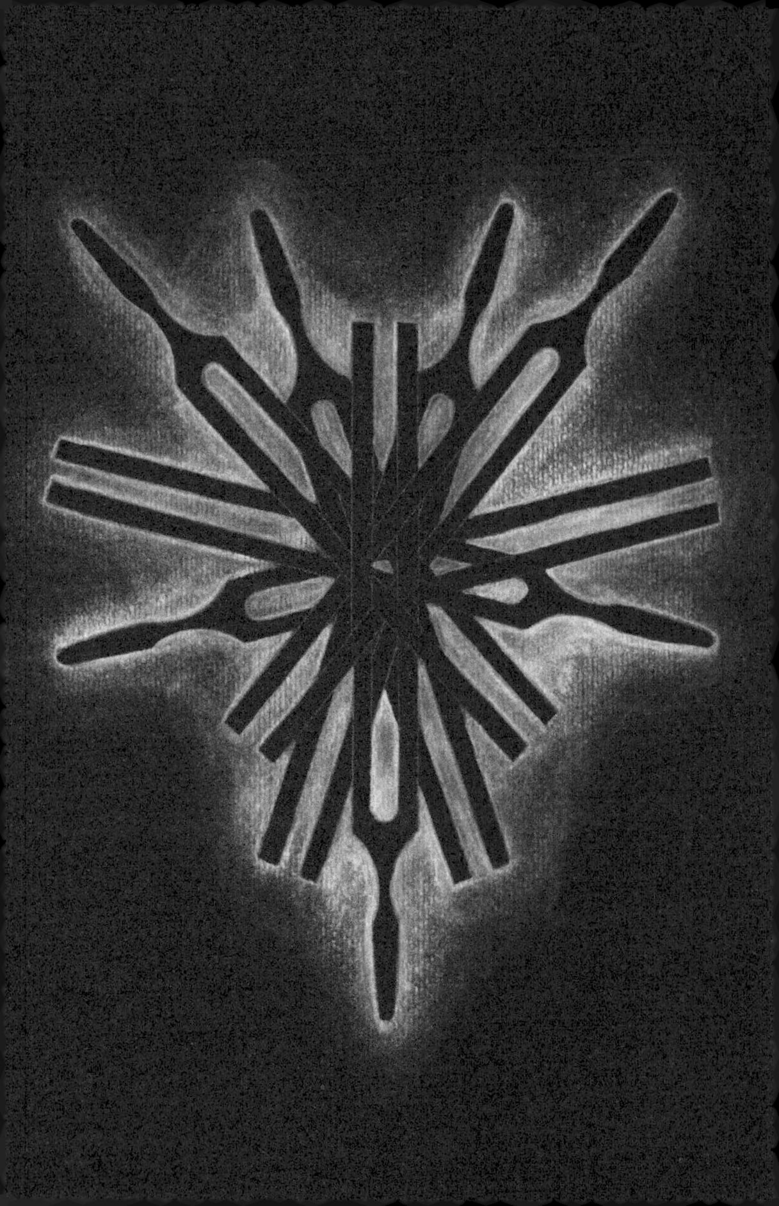

Quantum Listening

From Practice to Theory (to Practice Practice)

PAULINE OLIVEROS

'Through the practice of meditation we can explore the depth of insight through the wisdom of listening and hearing.' Sogyal Rinpoche

From childhood I have practiced listening.

As a musician, I am interested in the sensual nature of sound, its power of synchronization, coordination, release and change. Hearing represents the primary sense organ – hearing happens involuntarily. Listening is a voluntary process that through training and experience produces culture.

All cultures develop through ways of listening.

Deep Listening is listening in every possible way, to everything it's possible to hear, no matter what you are doing. Such intense listening includes the sounds of daily life, of nature, or one's own thoughts, as well as musical sounds.

Deep Listening represents a heightened state of awareness and connects to all that there is. As a composer I make my music through Deep Listening.

Deep Listening is active.

What is heard is changed by listening and changes the listener. I call this the 'listening effect' or how we process what we hear. Two modes of listening are available – focal and global. When both modes are utilized and balanced, there is connection with all that there is. Focal listening garners detail from any sound and global listening brings expansion through the whole field of sound.

Listening shapes culture, locally and universally.

Listening is directing attention to what is heard, gathering meaning, interpreting and deciding on action.

Quantum Listening is listening to more than one reality simultaneously.

Listening for the least differences possible to perceive – perception at the edge of the new. Jumping like an atom out of orbit to a new orbit – creating a new orbit – as an atom occupies both spaces at once one listens in both places at once. Mothers do this. One focuses on a point and changes that point by listening.

Quantum Listening is listening in as many ways as possible simultaneously – changing and being changed by the listening.

I see and hear life as a grand improvisation – I stay open to the world of possibilities for interplay in the quantum field with self and others – community – society – the world – the universe and beyond.

Our improvisations will soon include accelerated artificial evolution – hybrid humans – new beings born of technology – new challenges, consequences, dangers, freedoms and responsibilities – all of this in addition to the life we lead through the habits of our own traditions.

How will we meet the genius of more rapidly evolving interactive cultures? A genius of culture that could give us freedom of perception, physical and mental limitations.

Will we stop the evolution with destruction and annihilation? Or embrace it courageously, to go forward into the new world we are creating, with all its edges?

Here follows a brief history and description of my practice called Deep Listening. I also describe Quantum Listening, a theory derived from the practice of Deep Listening. My composing, performing and educating are rooted in my practice and theory.

My theory of Quantum Listening leads back to practice practice!

As a composer and performer I have experienced a relationship with music technology that spans more than half a century. Technology is changing – and changing cultures

– more rapidly now than ever before. What used to take 300 years now happens in twenty minutes.

The time span of my teaching stretches fifty years, from the first lessons I taught to my accordion students at age fifteen to the more recent graduate composition seminars that I have given at Mills College as Darius Milhaud Professor, Oberlin Conservatory as professor of composition and other institutions.

Teaching has always engaged me, given back to me generously and nourished my career as a composer/performer.

When I taught 'The Nature of Music' to large classes of non-music majors at the University of California in San Diego, I wanted to engage the students in creative sound experiences. I began to compose pieces that would allow anyone to participate, whether they could read music or not. By 1970, I had begun to compose Sonic Meditations,[5] pieces based on the structure of human attention. Sonic Meditations gave my work a whole new direction. I began to understand just how important listening is to creative music making. Compared with reading and writing, relatively little attention is given to developing listening skills, or even to considering the nature of listening.

5. Pauline Oliveros, *Sonic Meditations*, Smith Publications, 1974.

I have been training myself to listen with a very simple meditation since 1953, when my mother gave me a tape recorder for my twenty-first birthday. The tape recorder had just become available on the home market and was not so ubiquitous as it is today. I immediately began to record from my apartment window whatever was happening. I noticed that the microphone was picking up sounds that I had not heard while the recording was in progress. I said to myself then and there:

'Listen to everything all the time and remind yourself when you are not listening.'

I have been practicing this meditation ever since more or less successfully. I still get the reminders after forty-six years. My listening continues to evolve as a lifelong practice.

How we listen creates our life. Listening is the basis of all culture.

The quality and flexibility of listening skills is the foundation of musicianship. The essence of musicianship is the ability to discern the smallest change in pitch or tempo, and relate that discernment to a field of ongoing sound or musical relationships.

For audiences the greatest gift is rapt attention.

Composing Sonic Meditations led me deeper into my listening practice and to the notion that there were other important ways to relate to teaching that were different from the presentation to students of prescribed and measurable content. Sonic Meditations helped me devise ways to engage students in creative sound making. Processing the results with discussion led to content that came from the inside out (student to professor) rather than exclusively from the outside in (professor to student).

As my work progressed in composition and performance, I came to the notion of Deep Listening. In 1988, together with Stuart Dempster and Panaiotis, I made a recording in an underground cistern in Washington State. The recording was released in 1989 by New Albion (NA 022 CD) under the title 'Deep Listening'.[6] Quoting from my CD liner notes:

> Each composer represented in Deep Listening has a very individual style of composition. As we improvise together, and listen intensely to one another, our styles encounter in the moment, and intermingle to make a collective music. I call the result deep listening.

After writing these words many activities began to unfold as Deep Listening.

In 1990 I published *Deep Listening Pieces,*[7] which contains a brief explanation of my listening theory. It involves two

6. Pauline Oliveros, Stuart Dempster, Panaiotis, *Deep Listening*, New Albion (NA 022 CD).
7. Pauline Oliveros *Deep Listening Pieces*, Deep Listening Publications, 1990.

attention processes, focal and global listening, and the interdependence of the two modes.

In 1991, together with Heloise Gold – tai chi master and choreographer – I created and led the first Deep Listening Retreat at Rose Mountain Retreat Center. I had already done research at the Center for Music Experiment at the University of California in 1973 and given numerous workshops based on my Sonic Meditations. This research is detailed in several articles in my book *Software for People*.[8]

The retreat form I devised gave me a wonderful opportunity to focus the material and to work more intensively with people. After five years it was clear that advanced work was needed for those returning every year.

Poet and psychotherapist IONE joined Deep Listening as an instructor to offer 'Listening Through Dreaming',[9] giving participants the opportunity to practice listening in the retreat twenty-four hours a day.

Based on a request from one of the participants, I decided to offer an advanced retreat and a three-year certificate program for those who would like to teach Deep Listening and use it as a guide for their own creative development.

8. Pauline Oliveros, *Software for People*, Smith Publications, 1984.
9. IONE, *'Is This A Dream?' Workshop Manual*, Ministry of Maat Publications, 1997.

As a team, IONE, Heloise Gold and I unified our teaching with listening.

Consilient common ground creates a whole learning situation. The retreat is always held in a beautiful, natural mountain environment. Tai chi and qi gong inform and ground the body in the ancient way of the Tao. Dream incubation and processing bring the aura of dreams into interplay with waking consciousness; sounding and responding through Deep Listening provide new portals to creativity, unity with self and others.

What Is Deep Listening?

For me, Deep Listening is a lifelong practice. The more I listen, the more I learn to listen. Deep Listening involves going below the surface of what is heard, expanding to the whole field of sound while finding focus. This is the way to connect with the acoustic environment, all that inhabits it and all that there is.

For others, Deep Listening is a practice consisting of listening and sounding exercises and pieces that I and others have composed since 1970. The results are processed by group discussions in workshops and retreats.

Deep Listening is for musicians as well as participants from other disciplines and interests. Previous musical training is not required.

The key to multi-level existence is Deep Listening – listening in as many ways as possible, to everything that can possibly be heard, all of the time. Deep Listening is exploring the relationships among any and all sounds, whether natural or technological, intended or unintended, real, remembered or imaginary. Thought is included.

Deep Listening includes all sounds expanding the boundaries of perception. In this concept is language and the nature of its sound, as well as natural sound and technological sound. Deep Listening also includes the environmental and atmospheric context of sound.

Listening is the key to performance.

Whatever the discipline, responses that originate from Deep Listening resonate with being – inform the artist and audience and make art an effortless harmony. Inclusiveness is essential to the process of unlocking layer after layer of imagination, meaning and memory down to the cellular level of human experience.

Hearing is the passive basis of listening.

Hearing is involuntary. Hearing protects us from unseen dangers. We can hear without listening. Unconsciousness: we choose to listen inwardly or outwardly to the past, present or future. Consciousness: listening actively directs one's attention to what is heard, to the interaction of the relationships of sounds and modes of attention.

We hear in order to listen.

We listen in order to interpret our world and experience meaning. Our world is a complex matrix of vibrating energy, matter and air, just as we are made of vibrations. Vibration connects us with all beings and connects us to all things interdependently.

We open in order to listen to the world as a field of possibilities and we listen with narrowed attention for specific things of vital interest to us in the world.

We interpret what we hear according to the way we listen.

Through accessing many forms of listening we grow and change whether we listen to the sounds of our daily lives, the environment or music.

Deep Listening takes us below the surface of our consciousness and helps to change or dissolve limiting boundaries.

Babies are the best Deep Listeners.

Think of the tremendous acts of attention and concentration that babies make to explore sounds and speak their first words, to learn language and communicate through listening.

Deep Listening is a birthright for all healthy humans.

As a blind person, the musician Stevie Wonder has listening abilities that persons with normal sight don't ordinarily develop. Stevie Wonder is a Deep Listener as many blind people are.

With heightened listening ability one can detect the slightest differences in sounds. This enables acute voice recognition, echo detection, spatial location, etc. Such heightened listening substitutes auralization for visualization (or seeing) by creating sonic pictures, and so on.

If you are a blind person, hearing is your means of sight, but such acute listening ability also could be cultivated among people with normal sight.

If you were a deaf person hearing for the first time with a newly implanted bionic ear, how would you know what you were hearing? You would have to learn to interpret the sounds.

What if you could hear like a bat zipping and swooping around the night sky, or a whale sounding the depths of the oceans, or elephants sounding the earth?

What would it be like to attend a live concert with the ability to hear it any way that you like?

What if you, as a sophisticated listener, could individually adjust and optimize the room acoustics for the music to your own taste?

What if you could equalize and mix an orchestra the way you want to hear it – while other listeners are hearing their own versions of the same concert?

What if you could cancel out any interference automatically so that only the music is purely audible?

What if such feats are possible as an internal and private experience? How could your experience be valued in relation to a community of interest?

What if your experience could be shared instantly in the present moment or later?

Audio engineers already do this; they have developed the art of recording concerts and usually have the best seat in the house for sound, which they hear through headphones or near field speakers. The results of their listening can be shared through recordings.

All the technology for controlling the sound of concert acoustics exists already.

What if you could hear the frequency of colors?

Research on visual simulations and robotic sight has far outpaced research on hearing. Hearing has not seemed as important to scientists and technologists as seeing. One hears repeatedly that we live in a 'visually oriented society' even though the ear tells the eye where to look.

Those of us who are aurally-oriented are marginalized.

For example: the $165 million dollar Mars Climate Orbiter probe launched by NASA in 1998 brought a $15 microphone from a hearing aid module along as a hitchhiker. This was an afterthought, though listening for the sounds of other worlds could yield data that might not come from cameras. We take cameras to the zoo, not tape recorders. And zoos are generally not open during prime sound time in the early morning or evening.

We need to be listening in all possible modes to meet the challenges of the unknown – the unexpected.

An unconscious, negative attitude that makes hearing less important than sight developed in parallel with industrial age technology. Pre-industrial cultures depended on hearing for survival. Now unnecessarily loud motor sounds serve to let the operator know that a machine is working. Silent machines are possible, but people seem to need the aural feedback even though it may contribute to the destruction of their hearing…

Why is industrial sound so often excessive?

Sound conveys a sense of power and connection to the machine operator. Sound is the mythos and symbolic representation of the need to accumulate power. It is an unconscious 'participation mystique'.

The sounds of machines dominate and are a constant, ubiquitous presence.

There is no courting of silence. Urban sound levels continue to rise in a great, cacophonic puzzle. Those who operate machines can feel powerful – in control.

No part of the planet is untouched by machine sound. No wonder that youth culture has embraced loud, amplified music. How else could they feel heard, extending their work to audiences as a powerful presence?

Technology has deeply altered the quality of life, both positively and negatively.

The devaluation of hearing through unconsciousness and ignorance has caused a serious imbalance in the quality of life. Suppression of listening is a consequence of this imbalance. Separation and alienation results. How we attend to this imbalance will have a profound influence on the future of human values. How we use the power of sound and music affects our values.

We need sound designers and composers as consultants to city planning and noise abatement regulation.

Machines such as cranes, earth movers, pile drivers, and so on, have amplified human muscle power enormously in the Industrial Age and enabled the large building accomplishments in the development of cities. We have machines that multiply and leverage our senses and our mental capabilities. In the twenty-first century we will be grappling with who we are as extended humans – hybrid computer/humans and computer beings.

We already see and hear far into outer space and into micro space.

With the Hubble telescope we are able to see into galaxies from the edge of the universe. How thrilling it would be if we could hear this, too? How about launching a parabolic microphone on the next satellite to listen for the music of the spheres? With the electron microscope we can see atomic structures, but we could also listen to the micro-world, hearing a strange universe unfolded by quantum mechanics.

Research on hearing and repairing damaged ears increased after World War II, whereas the need for ear protection in the workplace had not been recognized earlier. Hearing loss is usually a slow, painless process occurring over many years and not necessarily detected until late in its progression. When veterans returned from battle with acoustic trauma, the more instant damage from the loud explosions of war motivated the Army to do new research on protecting and repairing ears.

In 1978 the first person who was implanted with a bionic ear, Rod Saunders, went profoundly deaf because of head injury, and received the bionic ear when he was forty-eight years old. The prototype bionic ear (a cochlear transplant) proved to be a success and was commercialized in 1982. A range of improvements over the years, as a result of the continuing research, has led to additional benefits for people like Rod. Research from the University of Melbourne has found that over 20,000 people throughout the world can hear because of the bionic ear, including over 10,000 children.

At least 28 million people in the United States suffer hearing loss. Sixty per cent have genetic hearing loss and the rest have damaged ears from industrial noise and loud music. At least 16 million are under thirty years old.[10]

Ignorance (more than accidents) causes ear damage, which is currently irreversible. All the devices that are supposed to contribute positively to the quality of life are dangerous if they also produce sound levels at and above 85db and people have more or less continuous exposure to those levels.

10. National Institutes of Health, Consensus Development Conference on Noise and Hearing Loss.

Many people, especially young people, have not a clue as to the danger of loud music through headphones, at a disco or concert.

People are not necessarily aware of the occupational hazards of loud motors, although some progress has been made. Workplace ethics should hold employers accountable for such hazardous sounds. Manufacturers should be accountable too.

Musicians need education about the dangers of their profession.

Audiologists should be consulted routinely and should hold positions as health inspectors. Just as restaurants must maintain cleanliness against infectious microbes, industrial workplaces should be free of continuous sound above 85db. Ear protection should be provided for employees.

Interpretation of our sense information (listening) and the sharing of this experience with each other is the basis of culture and our values.

For example, the members of traditional musical ensembles share knowledge through the experience of performing together, interpreting and creating repertoire and sharing it with audiences. Audiences participate by responding to the music. We rejoice in the pleasure of music that we know and love. Community develops around music. Critical response, discernment and education helps to shape and conserve musical values.

Unfamiliar contemporary music tests values, challenges habits, helps to create new thought patterns and expanded awareness. We need an improvatory of music[11] to balance the conservatory and promote the creation of music.

Youth culture is transforming music and creating new values across cultural divides. DJs are remixing the artifacts of recorded music cultures as performances. They are listening differently. They are deconstructing recorded music and turning recorded sound into live performance. The movement is powerful and reaches others instantly through the internet, as well as other media venues. Their listening and cultural flexibility is the future of music.

My own work is now presented live on the internet. Fifty years ago I performed for the first time on another new media venue – television. Now, in the twenty-first century, the youth culture will navigate this new internet venue.

We have arrived at the threshold of the twenty-first century with sense organs developed gradually by natural

11. Pauline Oliveros, 'Quantum Improvisation: The Cybernetic Presence', Improvisation Across Borders Conference, UCSD, 1999.

selection through the slow millennial process of evolution. We assume that as humans we hear in the same manner, although not all ears have the same acuity.

And, because we do not all share the same culture, we definitely are not all listening in the same way with the same attention.

Soon we will be faced with an unprecedented, exponential acceleration in technology.

How do we understand normal hearing? What are we listening for?

Restoration of damaged sense organs and nerves will be possible. Regeneration of nerves may be possible also. For the first time, there may also be a choice for enhancement of sense organs and for new perceptual abilities, if our brains can handle the processing involved with the unfamiliar. When we cannot process complex information we tend to shut down our senses and retreat.

What if such retreat was impossible?

What if we could share our thoughts instantly over a network as computers now do? Such possibilities and amplified intelligence will present new challenges to our ethics and future human values.

What would you want to hear if you had a bionic ear that could let you listen to anything, anywhere, any time?

As a musician would you like to focus on a particular instrument in an orchestra that seems inaudible? Or listen globally, with the ability to equalize and optimize the sound of the whole ensemble, canceling out any distracting interferences?

What does a bat hear as it swoops and dives through the air, sounding its prey to locate it?

Would you like to zoom into a waterfall to hear individual sounds of the falling drops? Would you like to hear the sound of a cell dividing in your own body? The sound of blood coursing through your veins as you monitor your own health?

How about discerning the exact distance of sounds with an internal molecular computer?

What are the sounds of the gasses in deep space?

All of this enhancement to hearing is already available with outboard equipment: microphones, amplifiers, speakers.

Surveillance by spies is quite sophisticated.

What if such equipment were available as onboard, internal equipment through microscopic, ingested technology? (Never mind implants – they will be outdated.) How would you want to use your newly enhanced ear power? How could humanity handle such power?

What is microscopic ingested technology?

According to Ray Kurzweil, nanobots are microscopic-sized robots which will exist by 2030.[12] Entering the bloodstream, nanobots could scan your brain from the inside. Nanobots could swim through every capillary of your brain and take a high-resolution picture from inside.

Note that Kurzweil doesn't posit nanobots that listen.

Nanotechnology is underway. The result could mean that new neural networks could be created and controlled within the brain. Nerves could be repaired. Brain extenders could extend your pattern recognition and memory. You would have the processing power of powerful computers or return to normal, carbon-based being.

Kurzweil predicts: 'In a hundred years there may be no clear distinction between humans and computers. There will be enormous augmentation of human perceptual and cognitive abilities through neural implant technology. Humans who do not use such implants (or nanobots) are unable to participate in meaningful dialogue with those who do – knowledge is understood instantaneously through assimilated knowledge protocols. The goal of education and intelligent beings is discovering new knowledge to learn.'[13]

12. Ray Kurzweil interviewed by Virginia Lee for comngrnd.com.

13. Ray Kurzweil, *The Age of Spiritual Machines: When Computers Exceed Human Intelligence*, Viking, 1999.

What about spirituality?

To Kurzweil a spiritual experience is 'a pattern of information.'[14]

For Matthew Fox, 'spirituality by definition means plummeting to the depths, getting down to the realm of experience. Spirituality is about living deeply. It puts experience before everything else. It's about responding with passion, awe, reverence and gratitude to everything in life – including the grief, the pain, the suffering, the injustice. It's about tasting God, not just talking about God.'[15]

We will need all the wisdom that we can possibly absorb to deal morally and ethically with the powers inherent in nanotechnology. Our battles with good and evil will jump to a new level.

Enter the Chip Monk![16] Will spirituality evolve on a microchip with the programed essence of the best of our world religions available to all? Could the Chip Monk be ingested to assist one's inner monk in the practice of deep ecumenism and the distillation of universal truth?

If you are a Buddhist, listening leads to the 'Buddhaverse'; if you are a Christian, listening leads you to the word of God;

14. Ray Kurzweil interviewed by Virginia Lee for comngrnd.com.
15. Matthew Fox interviewed by Virginia Lee for comngrnd.com.
16. Chip Monk was contributed by Stuart Dempster.

if you are an artist, listening leads you to your material and to shape the material. If you are a scientist, listening leads you to theory and experiment.

If you are a spy, listening may lead you to prison.

Quantum Listening leads you to notice that you are listening. Quantum Listening leads you to attention to a point – all or nothing focus which changes that point forever.

Quantum Listening leads you to an all-embracing perspective of an ever-expanding field.

We live in these conditions and our listening simultaneously perceives and shapes the moments that we live whether we are Buddhist, Christian, Islamic, artist, scientist, or anything else. Whoever and whatever we are, religion is a set of rules and regulations for a particular kind of listening. Style in art sets the way of listening.

Quantum Listening is listening to our listening. The field expands to embrace all kinds of listening, with openness to all possibilities.

In 1990 the noted ethnomusicologist Ki Mantle Hood proposed the quantum theory of music. When asked for the formula for QTM in 1994, he replied: 'At present, our modus operandi is asking questions. We try to identify neglected, overlooked, not-always-obvious phenomena that relate in any way to the perception of music. That order of perception is only possible by participation.' Participation means actually experiencing all aspects of music creation and performance.

What is Quantum Listening?

Quantum Listening is listening in all sense modes to or for the least possible differences in any component part of a form or process while perceiving the whole and sensing change.

The Quantum Listener listens to listening.

Quantum Listening simultaneously creates and changes what is perceived. The perceiver and the perceived co-create through the listening effect. All sounds are included in the field. This creates potential, cultivates surprises, opens the imagination and approaches and even plunges over the edges of perception into the mystery of the universe predicted by quantum field theory.

Quantum Listening is the ability to discern all that there is in a single moment – point in space (a transient) or a quanta.

'In the new physics of quantum field theory, particles have an 'aura' or a force field. Although it cannot be seen, its presence is felt. It conveys forces from one particle to another as they interact.'[17]

Analogously, when one is listening to the whole field of sound without focusing on any one sound but expanding to

17. P. Steven Petersen, *The Quantum Tai Chi*, Empyrean Quest, 1996.

include all sounds that can be heard – sounds seem to become interrelated rather than chaotic or meaningless – the field conveys forces (energy) from one sound to another.

The field seems to have a unified logic and form as if it were a composed piece of music.

'What is a field? A field carries the potential for manifesting a force. Particles of objects inside a field may change or move.'[18]

The field of sound can be felt as potential force. There is active participation by the listener and co-creation of this form between the listener and sounds.

The field assumes meaning (potential force) and is transformed by the listener. The listener is also transformed by the field. If one is not listening in this expanded way then the form disappears into the background of consciousness – the field disappears – is meaningless, attention narrows, the potential lessens. This is analogous to the collapse of the wave function in quantum mechanics when a particle is observed and decides to change state.

Within the 'listening field' sounds which shift and change inside the field are the manifestation of forces which give rise to the perceived form. Listeners will hear the form slightly

18. Ibid.

differently each from their own angle of observation in the field. Different listeners would have to occupy different locations in the field thus their experience of the field would be different. This is no less true when listening to a piece of music in an audience in a concert hall.

A quantum theory of music as proposed in 1990 by Ki Mantle Hood would have to account for these slight differences in perception, their interaction and effect.

Each listener, through the act of listening, affects the field and thus the form. The form affects the listener in a dance of reflections in the space between.

Listening performers feel the 'listening effect' as they are performing for an audience.

This is focal/global listening with the added perspective of a 'witness' function.

This is listening to listening – layers of processing in the brain and body.

The skin listens too.

In fact the whole body listens in this heightened state of awareness. which can expand continually unless attention narrows (perhaps to ego concerns) and there is the collapse of the wave function and a change in the field and its potential.

While practicing qi gong I have experienced listening with the palms of my hands to sense these electromagnetic fields. Since these are vibrations, I call this sensing listening with the palms of the hands. Simply imagining the sound of humming transfers immediately to the palms of my hands and manifests as healing energy.

There is a deep relationship between qi gong and quantum field theory.

According to the speculation of physicist E. H. Walker:

> Consciousness may be associated with all quantum mechanical processes – since everything that occurs is ultimately the result of one or more quantum mechanical events, the universe is 'inhabited' by an almost unlimited number of rather discrete, conscious entities that are responsible for the detailed workings of the universe.[19]

Can sounds be understood as particles?

> In a fashion analogous to auric fields, particle fields influence certain particles when near them.[20]

Sounds near one another influence each other. Listeners near one another affect or influence one another with active listening.

> Particles have auras. This makes them like everything else in the universe, as the ancient Chinese viewed it.[21]

19. Evan Harris Walker, 'The Nature of Consciousness', *Mathematical Biosciences*, Vol. 7, 1970.
20. P. Steven Petersen.
21. Ibid.

Photons (light particles), do appear to process information and to act accordingly, and therefore, strange as it may sound, they seem to be organic.[22]

Particles behave like they have consciousness.[23]

In fact, modern Quantum Field Theory suggests that what we call a particle is an 'energy knot' in the field . . . Thus particles are a flow creating the illusion of a form, made up of concentrated 'qi' . . . 'Qi' is similar to a cloud.[24]

When the Chi [qi] condenses, its visibility (or audibility) becomes apparent so that there are then the shapes (of individual things {or sounds}). When it disperses its visibility (or audibility) is no longer apparent and there are no shapes (or sounds). At the time of its condensation, can one say otherwise than that this was but temporary? But at the time of its dispersing, can one hastily say that is then non existent?[25]

Is sound intelligent? Does sound have consciousness?

Listen to sound disappearing. This meditation that I practice takes one to the border of reality and virtuality. When do you stop hearing the sound? When does memory begin?

What we hear depends on the angle from which our ear receives sound. How we listen depends on our consciousness.

22. Gary Zukav, *The Dancing Wu Li Masters*, Bantam Books, 1979.
23. P. Steven Petersen.
24. Hermann Weyl, *Philosophy of Mathematics and Natural Science*, Princeton, 1949.
25. Chang Tsai, quoted in Fung Yu-Lan, *A Short History of Chinese Philosophy*, Free Press, 1997.

Are we creating the sound that we hear by listening or is sound creating our listening? Is it co-creation between consciousnesses? Is the sound disappearing or am I disappearing?

Human values are developed through the experience of listening. With practice, humanity could be transformed to a flexible culture of listeners.

Listening involves a reciprocity of energy flow; exchange of energy; sympathetic vibration: tuning into the web of mutually supportive interconnected thoughts, feelings, dreams, vital forces comprising our lives; empathy; the basis for compassion and love.

Yes, Deep Listening is the foundation for a radically transformed social matrix in which compassion and love are the core motivating principles guiding creative decision making and our actions in the world.

Quantum Listening is a 'simple' practice, open to all, which has profoundly rich and far-flung implications for bringing to our world the two conditions the Dalai Lama illuminates in his recent book *Ethics for the New Millennium*: happiness and relief of suffering.[26]

The practice generates theory.

26. With thanks to Norman Lowrey, Professor of Composition at Drew University and Deep Listening practitioner, for this contribution.

Theory is perceiving structure – analyzing and explaining structure so that testing and experiments (practice) can be done. Theory directs practice and creates culture to practice practice.

Practice is a way of action – a set or sets of ways of doing or responding to gain experience

Listeners practicing cultural flexibility[27] would be aware of the profound interdependence of all beings and all things. A new music reflective of a new humanity with a high value on life could arise.

Pauline Oliveros

Oakland, CA

9 December 1999

27. 'Cultural flexibility' was contributed by Abbie Conant in conversation with the author.

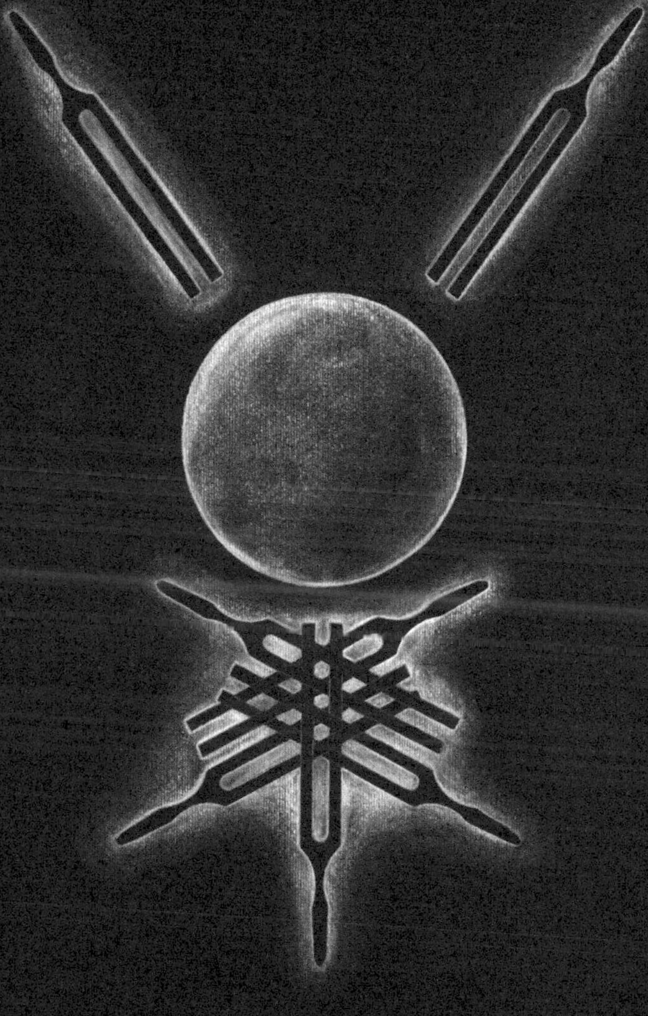

Compassion

Inspired by the Sonic Meditations of Pauline Oliveros

Alison Johns, Mills College, Oakland, CA. Fall 1999.

1. All musicians should sit in a circle, facing one another.
2. Close your eyes.
3. Imagine a cord that leads from the base of your spine all the way to the center of the earth.
4. Take a deep breath, and as you release the breath, follow the cord all the way down. Imagine its color, shape and pathway. Hum or sing the sound of this journey to the center of the earth.
5. Connect the cord firmly to the earth's center.
6. When you have done this, stay on the pitch that you are making.
7. Hold your tone until everyone is singing or humming their own, unique tone.
8. When everyone is firmly connected, send a tone swirling clockwise around the circle. Anyone can start.
9. Match the sound of the person to your left, then change it, then match it again. Have fun.
10. When you all are ready, send a tone of peace to all the beings in the building.

11. Extend that tone of peace to the campus.
12. Expand the circle to your city.
13. Ever outwards to your country.
14. Next to your continent.
15. And finally to the planet.
16. Enjoy.
17. When all are ready, bring the sound back to the room, back to the circle.
18. Find a common tone.
19. End when it's finished.
20. Be sure that you touch the ground with your hands when you stand up again.

Bibliography

George Lipsitz, *Dangerous Crossroads: Popular Music, Postmodernism and The Poetics of Place*, Verso Books, 1994

Richard Morris, *The Universe, The Eleventh Dimension, and Everything: What We Know and How We Know It*, Four Walls Eight Windows, 1999

Pauline Oliveros, *The Roots of the Moment*, Drogue Press, 1998

Edward O. Wilson, *Consilience: The Unity of Knowledge*, Vintage, 1998

Webliography

http://iias.leidenuniv.nl/oideion/issues/issue2/articles/hood/frame o.html

http://www.zinezone.com/zones/digital/multimedia/kurzweil/interview6.html

http://www.jupiterscientific.org/science/baeparts/superstring.html

http://www.angelfire.com/hi2/UFOCHARTS/index.html

http://msnbc.com/news/202284.asp?cp1=1

http://www.neurosonics.com/bgm-kurzweil.html

http://www.comngrnd.com/houston.html

http://www.comngrnd.com/rinpoche.html

http://www.medoto.unimelb.edu.au/bei/history1.htm
http://www.militaryaudiology.org/bang/index.html
http://www.militaryaudiology.org/aric/index.htm

Hearing loss is one of the greatest health threats to military forces. Civilians would also benefit as noise-induced hearing loss has reached epidemic proportions in all industrialized nations.

Special thanks to all Deep Listeners and to:

H.E. Tai Situ Rinpoche
Monique Buzzarte
Abbie Conant
Stuart Dempster
Lester Ingber
IONE
Norman Lowrey
William Osborne
Jann Pasler
Alex Potts
Moira Roth
Juliet Shepherd
Bonnie Wright

Images by Aura Satz